Dorothy Tepera Palmer and Mary Sherek Tepera
Archlebov Czechoslovakia 1981

© 2013 All Rights Reserved. No part of this Publication may be reproduced in any form or by any means, including scanning, photocopying, or otherwise without prior written permission of the Copyright holder.

Published by PCG Publishing
http://pcgpublishing.weebly.com

Delicious Authentic Czech Kolache Recipes

Keep up with other books by this Author!
http://pcgpublishing.weebly.com

Visit the site to see upcoming cookbooks and others topics.

Enter to win a FREE copy of this cookbook!

Delicious Authentic Czech Kolache Recipes

Table of Contents

Chapter 1 – Introduction & Background 4

Chapter 2 - Let's start with some basics...7

   The Best Way to Use This Book..11

Chapter 3 – Step by Step Dough 12

Chapter 4 - Additional Kolache Dough Recipes..................................26

Chapter 5 – FILLINGS!...43

   Apricot Filling 43

   Posýpka 43

   Poppy seed filling (from dry) 44

   Poppy seed filling (from can)...44

   Apple or Peach or Prune filling: 45

   Cottage cheese filling for open-faced kolaches 45

   Dry Cottage Cheese 46

   Cottage cheese filling for closed kolaches 47

   Cream Cheese Filling: 47

   Sausage Filling:...48

Chapter 6 - Left-Over Dough = Kačenky!..50

Chapter 7 - Videos 53

Dedication 54

About The Author 58

Delicious Authentic Czech Kolache Recipes

Chapter 1 – Introduction & Background

**Kolaches? Koláč, Koláče, Koláche, Koláčky
No matter how it's spelled, we think they taste <u>Great</u>!**

For those living in the Texas "Czech Belt", kolaches are a part of everyday life. They easily compete with strudel as the official State Pastry! This sweet yeast bread filled with fruit or cheese was brought to the U.S. with Czech immigrants, in the mid-1800s.

Delicious Authentic Czech Kolache Recipes

A kolache (KO-lah-ch, sg.), (KO-lah-chis, plural) [American spelling], for those who have never been blessed with a sampling of the pastry, is a type of pastry that holds a dollop of fruit rimmed by a puffy pillow of supple dough. The name of the pastry derives from the word *kola*, which means *round* in Czech, and the ending of the word defines a native sentimental attachment to the bun.

The traditional pastry was a key food eaten in Czech daily life and immigrants in the U.S. continued to eat kolaches to hold onto their Czech heritage and identity in a new land. Traditional fillings are prune, apricot, cheese, or poppyseed and they originated as a semisweet wedding dessert. In Texas there is a fierce competition between bakers and Czech bakeries... everyone claims theirs is the BEST!

As the years went by, Czech descendants began adding their own creativity on the traditional kolache and that is why you will find many different recipes and all kinds of flavors available, from pineapple to sausage and more.

Delicious Authentic Czech Kolache Recipes

You may find yourself outside the warm buttery embrace of the Texas Czech belt but you can still have authentic Texas-Czech kolaches by making them yourself!

Baking kolaches is one of the most popular Czech customs still handed down. I owned a Czech Bakery for 10 years and I will be sharing the recipes I used in the bakery for step-by-step directions in this book. This old world classic will be easy for you to make and be perfect every time!

Delicious Authentic Czech Kolache Recipes

Chapter 2 - Let's start with some basics...

The Name

In Czech the name for one pastry is koláč (KO-lah-ch). The plural is koláče (KO-lah-che).

For the purposes of this book I will use the American spelling kolache (KO-lah-ch) for one pastry and kolaches (KO-lah-chis) for plural.

Kolache Dough

Every Czech family has its' favorite dough recipe. I will use mine in this step-by-step direction. Mine is the only "refrigerated" kolache dough I have come across and has been handed down for over 100 years. I prefer it because it breaks up the work by allowing me to prepare the dough and fillings one day and finish the work and bake the next day. It takes a little longer to rise since the dough is starting out cold. I offer many other dough recipes in this book. Try them all and pick your favorite!

Kolache dough is a light and sweet dough you can use for many different purposes. It makes wonderful dinner rolls or even a loaf similar to Hawaiian bread.

Kolache Shape

The traditional shape is round with the filling in a center well (open-faced). The closer you set them on the pan, the more "square" they will be. Another option is enclosing the filling within the dough. We will be doing both. My mother made "open-faced" kolaches using fruit filling but she enclosed the fillings of cottage cheese or poppyseed inside the dough.

There is also another shape where you flatten the dough, place the filling in the center, bring together the four corners over the filling, and then attach the dough together on top. This is not so common in Texas.

My mom would use leftover dough, tie it in a knot and bake it. She called these kačenky (KA-chen-kee) or "baby ducks" because that is what they looked like. She would sprinkle sugar on them or even ice them with a thin powdered-sugar icing and I loved them as a child... still do!

Delicious Authentic Czech Kolache Recipes

Fillings

When making fruit kolaches always start with dried fruit. Pie fillings or jams are too runny for kolaches. Poppyseed is difficult to get in bulk and then you have to grind it and cook it, and cool it. Not many people have a poppyseed grinder lying around. You can get poppyseed in a can and ready to use in most large grocery stores. Look in the pie filling area. The brand I am most familiar with is *Solo*.

Sausage kolaches are distinctly an American invention but they are much loved by most kolache aficionados. Even though most people call them "kolaches" they are actually klobasniky (KLO-bahs-nyee-kee). You can use any type of pre-cooked sausage you want. Try to use one with a casing that is easy to chew. Even Little Smokies work well. It doesn't have to be sausage… you can use sliced ham and even add cheese. Be creative!

Kolache Toppings

You have a choice here too. As I was growing up, the only topping for kolaches I was familiar with was posýpka (PO-seep-ka). It is a crumb

Delicious Authentic Czech Kolache Recipes

mixture of flour, sugar, and butter placed on top of the filling before baking.

When I had my bakery I made a powdered sugar/water mixture and put it in a squeeze bottle. I then squeezed this glaze on top of the kolaches in a zigzag pattern. I also see some bakers dusting the finished kolache with powdered sugar, and of course, I see a lot with no topping.

Abbreviations Used

tsp = teaspoon

TBL = tablespoon

1 envelope of dry yeast = ¼ oz. = 2 ¼ tsp. = 1 cake of fresh yeast (0.6 oz.)

All temperatures given in °F

Delicious Authentic Czech Kolache Recipes

The Best Way to Use This Book

If you are a novice, read the entire Chapter 3. It details the steps needed to make authentic Kolaches. Watch all the available videos. Especially watch the complete Video "Kolaches" at:

> http://youtu.be/j9TgcHSC_hY

Once your know how to make the dough and how to form and fill the kolaches, you can try additional dough recipes in Chapter 4 and additional filling recipes in Chapter 5.

Delicious Authentic Czech Kolache Recipes

Chapter 3 – Step by Step Dough

My Kolache Dough

Preparation time: 30 minutes

Ingredients:

3 packages yeast (total of ¾ oz. or 21g)
2 tsp sugar
2/3 cup warm water (not hot, should be around 100-115 °F)

4 eggs
1 cup butter, melted

1 cup evaporated milk
1 cup whole milk
1 cup sugar
2 tsp salt

9 cups flour

Additional melted butter to brush containers, pans and dough.

12

Delicious Authentic Czech Kolache Recipes

Instructions:

The Day Before –
    1. Make the Dough &
    2. Make the Fillings

1.   Make the Dough

Figure 3.1 – Gather everything to make the dough.

1. In a medium sized bowl, place the yeast, sugar, and warm water. Stir to mix then set aside. By the time you use it, the mixture should be foamy. You may want to do this at least 15 minutes before you start making the dough.

Delicious Authentic Czech Kolache Recipes

2. Break eggs into a large bowl. Beat eggs and add 1 cup sugar slowly, beating well. Add can milk, whole milk, melted butter, and salt. Mix well.

3. Add yeast mixture and mix together.

4. Add about half the flour and mix well with an electric mixer on low.

5. Continue adding the remaining flour 1 cup at a time, mixing well after each addition, until all the flour is used. Toward the end you will have to mix in the flour by hand. It will be too thick to use the mixer unless you are using one with a dough hook.

6. Scrape the dough into a large, buttered, sealable container. Lightly butter the top of the dough and the inside of the lid. Let it rest and rise for a while (30 minutes to 1 hour) covered with a clean dishtowel. (Do not seal it while it is rising.)

7. Close the container and place it in the refrigerator overnight.

Delicious Authentic Czech Kolache Recipes

TIP!

This dough keeps well in the refrigerator for a few days. As you need the dough, remove a portion, leaving the remainder in the refrigerator.

If you would like to see a video of me making this dough, you can see it on YouTube at...

http://youtu.be/K_gwIZkPACQ

2. Prepare Fillings:

Prepare as many of the fillings you want to use the next day to fill your kolaches. For you *First-Timers*, may I recommend...

> Cream Cheese (page 44)
> Apricot (page 40)
> Sausage (page 44)

Prepare some Posýpka (page 40) if you plan to use it.

Delicious Authentic Czech Kolache Recipes

The Next Day - Shape the Kolaches

Time required: 3 to 4 hours

If you would like to see a complete video of me making the following kolaches: shaping, filling, and baking, you can see it on YouTube at...

http://youtu.be/j9TgcHSC_hY

Figure 3.2 – Gather everything needed to shape and fill the kolaches.

Delicious Authentic Czech Kolache Recipes

1. Lightly flour your work surface and scrape some of the dough out of the container onto it.

2. Lightly flour the top of the dough and roll out to about 1 to 1 ½ in thickness.

3. Use the flat side of a scraper to cut the dough into squares.

TIP!

The first few times you make kolaches I recommend you use a small kitchen scale so that the dough pieces will be uniform in size. Soon, with practice, you will be able to make them uniform by sight or by feel.

Instead of rolling out the dough, you can simply scoop uniform sizes (about the size of a medium egg) out of the bowl using a spoon.

4. Add dough to, or take dough away from each piece of dough to make them all about 1.75 oz.

5. Flour your hands, pick up a piece of dough and roll firmly in the center of your hand, gradually relieving pressure by cupping your palms.

Delicious Authentic Czech Kolache Recipes

You should end up with a smooth ball of dough. This is usually the hardest part for beginners. Practice, practice, practice, until you have a smooth ball of dough. The most common mistake is not using enough pressure at the beginning of the balling process.

If you would like to watch me make Kolache Balls you can see it on YouTube at...

Video Available! **http://youtu.be/yVYcbhOP5Hs**

6. Place the balls of dough on a buttered baking sheet about 2 inches apart.

7. Butter the tops and sides of each ball.

8. Set in warm area and allow to rise double in size.

TIP!

Optional ways you can help them rise: You can set them on the counter if the weather is warm. You can place the pan in an oven (don't turn it on!) and place a pot of hot water in the oven with it. Or, you can line up the pans on your counter and hang a heating lamp above them (the lamp should be 3 to 4 feet away from the pans.)

Delicious Authentic Czech Kolache Recipes

Fig 3.3 – Dough balls before rising.

Figure 3.4 – Dough balls have risen and are ready to be filled.

When the dough has risen to at least twice the original size, continue…

Flour your index fingers and press the center of each ball of dough. Keeping your fingers

Delicious Authentic Czech Kolache Recipes

floured, continue to press the dough and slightly spread out creating a pool area in the center of the dough. Don't be shy.

You can watch a short video clip of me punching down the dough balls at...

http://youtu.be/G2M5vq0xq_0

Video Available!

1. Allow the dough to rest and rise again for about 15-20 minutes.

2. Reinforce the "well" in the dough before filling.

Delicious Authentic Czech Kolache Recipes

Fig 3.5 – Dough balls ready to fill.

3. Fill the "well" in the dough with plenty of filling.

4. Place a pinch (about 1 to ½ tsp) of posýpka in the center of each kolache.

5. Set the pans aside again to let rise double in size.

Delicious Authentic Czech Kolache Recipes

Figure 3.6 – Filled kolaches ready to bake.

6. Bake in a preheated oven at 375° and bake about 15-19 minutes. Bake on the bottom

Delicious Authentic Czech Kolache Recipes

rack for 9 minutes then place on the top rack the remainder of the time.

TIP!

My mom always said kolaches were under-baked if the bottoms were not browned. That is why I start mine on the bottom oven rack so the bottoms will be sure to brown. All ovens are different and you know yours best. The goal is to have the tops and bottoms lightly browned.

7. When the tops are nicely browned and the baking is done, remove the pans and butter the tops of the kolaches.

Figure 3.7 – Baked filled kolaches

Delicious Authentic Czech Kolache Recipes

Figure 3.8 – Filled and baked Cheese Kolaches

8. Let cool in pans for about 10 minutes then remove and separate to cooling racks until completely cool.

9. Store in sealable containers. You can freeze them also in sealable containers.

Congratulations! You have just completed making your first batch of kolaches!

Delicious Authentic Czech Kolache Recipes

Available YouTube Videos of this process:

1. Making sausage kolaches:

    http://youtu.be/TVBwWrW_5Gg

2. Making filled kolaches:

    http://youtu.be/u3GK406AMGk

3. Making Kačenky:

    http://youtu.be/aljVnqD1yuk

Delicious Authentic Czech Kolache Recipes

Chapter 4 - Additional Kolache Dough Recipes

All of the following kolache dough recipes were given to me by family and friends. We tested all of them before selecting the previous one for the bakery.

Classic Kolache Dough

Ingredients

3 packages dry yeast
½ cup warm water (100-115°F)
1 tsp sugar
1 cup butter (melted)
¾ cup sugar
3 egg yolks
2 ¾ cups milk (warm)
7 cups flour (more or less as needed)
3 tsp salt

Instructions:

Delicious Authentic Czech Kolache Recipes

1. Dissolve yeast in the ½ cup warm water and sprinkle 1 tsp sugar in a medium bowl. Set aside.

2. In a large bowl, cream sugar and butter, add egg yolks, salt and mix well.

3. Add the dissolved yeast mixture, 1 cup flour, and mix slowly with an electric mixer.

4. Add the warm milk and continue adding as much of the remaining flour as you can mix in with a large wooden spoon.

5. Knead in enough of the remaining flour to make a moderately soft dough.

6. Continue kneading until smooth and elastic (about 5 minutes)

7. Shape into a ball and place dough in a lightly buttered bowl, turn once to butter other surface.

8. Cover with a clean dishtowel. Let rise until double in size (1 to 1 ½ hours)

Delicious Authentic Czech Kolache Recipes

9. Punch down and turn out onto lightly floured work surface.

10. Pinch off egg size portions and roll into a ball using the palm of your hands in a circular motion.

11. Place about 1 inch apart on buttered pans.

12. Brush kolaches with melted butter, cover with a cloth, and let rise until double in size (about 1 hour).

Delicious Authentic Czech Kolache Recipes

Buttermilk Kolache Dough

Ingredients

3 ½ cups buttermilk 1 ¾
4 packages yeast 1 oz 4 ½ tsp
1 cup sugar ½
1 cup butter, margarine, or shortening ½
4 large eggs 2
½ cup water ¼
3 tsp salt 1 ½ tea
12 cups flour (more or less as needed) 6

Instructions:

1. Place lukewarm buttermilk in a large bowl. Add yeast and sprinkle with sugar (2 TB). Set aside for about 15 minutes or until yeast mixture is foamy.

2. In the meantime, beat eggs and sugar together until thick. Add to the yeast mixture.

3. Add salt and half the flour and mix well.

4. Add melted margarine (or shortening).

Delicious Authentic Czech Kolache Recipes

5. Continue adding remaining flour until you have a smooth dough.

6. Set aside in a warm place and let rise until double in bulk (about 1 hour but it depends on the temperature of the room). Punch it down and let it rise again.

7. Now the dough is ready to make into kolaches.

Delicious Authentic Czech Kolache Recipes

Šerek (SHARE-rek) Kolaches

2 packages yeast
1 tsp sugar
¼ cup warm water
¾ cup butter
¾ cup sugar
1 ½ cup evaporated milk
½ cup whole milk
2 egg yolks
2 tsp salt
6 cups flour (more or less as needed)

Instructions:

1. Dissolve yeast in the ¼ cup warm water. Sprinkle with 1 tsp sugar.

2. In a large bowl, cream sugar, margarine, egg yolks and salt. Mix well.

3. Add all the milk and the remaining flour, kneading in all the flour until you have a soft but not sticky dough.

4. Cover and let rise.

5. After dough has risen cut off small portions about the size of an egg. Shape into balls

Delicious Authentic Czech Kolache Recipes

and place on greased pans. Let rise until about double in size.

6. Make an indentation in each piece and place fruit filling in it. Sprinkle with posýpka if desired.

7. Bake at 375°F for about 15 minutes. When done, butter well.

Posýpka:
1 cup sugar
½ cup flour
¾ to 1 TB cinnamon
2 TB butter, melted
Mix all ingredients until it looks crumbly.

Delicious Authentic Czech Kolache Recipes

Award Winning Kolache Recipe

Ingredients

2 packages dry yeast
¼ cup warm water
1 tsp sugar
¾ cup shortening or butter
¾ cup sugar
2 egg yolks
2 cups milk (one 12 oz. can of evaporated milk plus warm water to equal 2 cups)
6 cups flour
2 tsp salt

Instructions:

1. Dissolve yeast in the ¼ cup of water and sprinkle with 1 tsp sugar.

2. In a large bowl, cream sugar and butter, add egg yolks, and salt. Mix well with a mixer.

3. Add the dissolved yeast and about ½ cup of the flour, mix slowly with the mixer.

4. Add the milk and continue adding the remaining flour, using the mixer then stir in

Delicious Authentic Czech Kolache Recipes

by hand with a large spoon until the dough is glossy and no longer sticky.

5. Cover dough and let rise in a warm place until double in size, about one hour (but it depends on the room temperature).

6. After dough has risen, cut off small portions of dough (about the size of an egg), using a tablespoon, shape into balls on greased pans about an inch apart.

7. Butter the balls of dough. Let rise until light. Make an indentation in each piece and place fruit inside.

8. Sprinkle with topping and bake in 425° for 15 minutes.

9. Butter the kolaches again after you remove them from the oven while they are still hot.

10. Remove onto a wire cooling rack. Seal in a plastic container when completely cool.

Delicious Authentic Czech Kolache Recipes

Czech Kolache Dough

Ingredients

2 packages active dry yeast
6 TB milk
1 tsp salt
2 TB sugar
½ cup butter, softened
4 whole eggs
4 egg yolks
4 cups flour

Instructions:

1. Heat the milk until warm (100-110°). Add yeast and let stand 10-15 minutes to dissolve.

2. Stir in salt and sugar.

3. In a large mixing bowl, put butter, 1 whole egg and 1 egg yolk. Beat with electric mixer. Continue adding 1 whole egg and 1 egg yolk, beating after each addition, until eggs are used up.

4. Mix in yeast. Add the flour.

Delicious Authentic Czech Kolache Recipes

5. Cover with a clean dish towel and place in a warm spot until double in size.

6. The dough is now ready to shape into balls then fill with your favorite filling.

Delicious Authentic Czech Kolache Recipes

Small Batch of Kolache Dough

Ingredients

2 packages dry yeast
1 tsp sugar
1/3 cup warm water

½ cup sugar
½ cup butter, melted
1 tsp salt
½ cup evaporated milk, warm
½ cup whole milk, warm

2 eggs
4 ½ cups flour

Instructions:

1. Place yeast, 1 tsp. sugar, and warm water in a small bowl to dissolve.

2. Mix together the sugar, butter, and salt. Add the milks.

3. Beat the eggs, add it to the yeast mixture, and then add the warm milk/butter mixture.

Delicious Authentic Czech Kolache Recipes

4. Add the flour and mix it all in, kneading all the flour in. The dough should be shiny, smooth, and not sticky.

5. Cover dough and let rise in warm spot for about an hour.

6. Form balls and fill with your favorite filling.

Delicious Authentic Czech Kolache Recipes

Aunt Frances Kolaches

Ingredients

2 cups whole milk, warm
2 TB yeast
¾ cups sugar
4 cups sifted flour

2 whole eggs
1 TB salt
¾ cup butter

Instructions:

1. Mix warm milk, yeast, sugar and 4 cups flour and let stand in a warm place approximately 45 minutes to an hour, until it rises.

2. Stir in the eggs, salt, and butter.

3. Mix well and add some sifted flour until it is stiff enough to work with yet soft.

4. Let the dough stand again after mixing this in.

Delicious Authentic Czech Kolache Recipes

5. Mix and let stand three more times. The total mixing process will take about 1 to 2 hours depending on how fast or slow your dough rises.

6. The dough is now ready to make kolaches.

7. Spoon out the dough one at a time onto a greased (buttered) cookie sheet.

8. Let the cut out dough rise (will take 15-30 minutes).

9. Stretch the centers of the kolaches with your fingers and put in your favorite filling.

10. Top the filling with posipka.

11. Brush kolaches with melted butter before putting in the oven.

12. Cook until brown at 375°F.

13. When done, brush with butter again.

14. Enjoy!

Delicious Authentic Czech Kolache Recipes

Grandma Sherek's Kolaches

Ingredients

3 eggs
4 tsp sugar
Pinch of salt
1/4 pound butter or margarine

¼ cup warm water
2 cakes of yeast
1 tsp sugar
1 ¾ cup milk

Instructions

1. Beat eggs, 4 tsp sugar, salt, and butter until foamy then let stand in warm place.

2. In a small bowl, mix together the warm water, yeast, 1 tsp of sugar and milk. Cover and let stand in warm place until foamy.

3. Mix together the yeast mixture and the egg mixture and add 2 cups of flour or more, as needed.

Delicious Authentic Czech Kolache Recipes

4. Let stand until risen to double the original size. Ready to make your favorite kolaches!

Delicious Authentic Czech Kolache Recipes

Chapter 5 – FILLINGS!

Apricot Filling

12 oz packaged dried apricots
2 cups sugar

> Place apricots in sauce pan, add water to cover. Cook slowly until fruit is soft (about 30 - 45 minutes).
>
> Mash with potato masher or electric mixer for about 3 minutes or until smooth. Add sugar. Cook slowly uncovered for 3 to 5 minutes, stirring constantly. Cool.

Posýpka

1 cup sugar
½ cup flour
2 TBL melted butter

> Mix all ingredients until mixture resembles coarse corn meal.

Delicious Authentic Czech Kolache Recipes

Poppy seed filling (from dry)

3 cups ground poppyseed
1 ½ cup sugar
2 TBL flour
1 ½ cup evaporated milk
1 tsp vanilla

Place the poppyseed, sugar, and flour in a pot and mix well. Add the milk and vanilla. Cook over medium and low heat until thick (about 10 to 15 minutes). Remove from heat and cool.

Dry poppy seed in bulk is hard to find. Poppyseed filling now can be purchased in cans at most large grocery stores. Most are ready to use. The brand I am familiar with is SOLO.

Poppy seed filling (from can)

You can absolutely use the can poppyseed filling just as it is from the can. I, however, prefer to "doctor" mine a little and it is hard to tell it was not home-ground and cooked:

For each can of SOLO Poppyseed Cake & Pastry Filling, I add:

Delicious Authentic Czech Kolache Recipes

¼ cup evaporated milk
2 TB sugar

> Simmer 15 minutes, mixing continuously.

Apple or Peach or Prune filling:

2 packages dried fruit
1 ½ cups sugar
3 TBL flour

> Cover dried fruit with water (about 3 cups). Cook until fruit is tender (about 30 minutes). Add sugar and flour. Cook until thickened. Try mashing softened fruit for a smoother filling. Cool.

Cottage cheese filling for open-faced kolaches

8 oz Cream cheese, softened
8 oz farmers cheese (dry cottage cheese)
¾ cup sugar
1 egg

Delicious Authentic Czech Kolache Recipes

¼ cup flour
1 tsp vanilla
½ cup raisins (optional)

> Mix all ingredients together. Refrigerate until ready to use.

Dry Cottage Cheese

If you cannot find dry cottage cheese you can make your own:

24 oz. (1 ½ lbs.) large curd cottage cheese

> Empty cottage cheese into a large sieve. Fill a bowl with water and set the sieve in it. Stir gently to wash the curds. Empty and refill water in bowl 2 or 3 times washing the curds gently each time.
>
> Remove the sieve from the bowl and place it over an empty bowl to drain for a few hours.
>
> This will yield about 2 cups (11 oz) of dry cottage cheese.

Delicious Authentic Czech Kolache Recipes

Cottage cheese filling for closed kolaches

2 cups Dry Cottage Cheese (recipe above)
¾ cup sugar
½ cup raisins

>Mix all ingredients together and refrigerate until ready to use.

>This filling is a little crumbly and harder to work with when enclosing it in kolache dough... but well worth it!

Cream Cheese Filling:

16 oz Cream Cheese
¾ cup sugar
1 egg
1 tsp vanilla

>Mix all ingredients together. Refrigerate until ready to use.

Delicious Authentic Czech Kolache Recipes

Sausage Filling:

Cook then cool the sausage. If you are using link sausage, cut sausage into 3 inch pieces and cut in half lengthwise so pieces will not be too fat. If the casing is too tough you can remove it (peel it off) before making the kolaches.

After your dough has been made and when it is ready to be shaped into kolaches, scoop out pieces of dough (about the size of an extra-large egg) using a spoon.

Flatten the dough with your fingers or a rolling pin. Place the sausage piece in the center of the flattened dough. Bring sides and ends up and completely seal by pressing the dough together.

If you would like to watch me make sausage kolaches, you can see it on YouTube at...

Video Available! http://youtu.be/TVBwWrW_5Gg

Place the sealed sausage kolaches (seam side down) on a buttered baking sheet about 1 inch apart.

Butter the surface of each kolache. Let sit for 30 minutes to one hour until the dough has risen and kolaches look puffy.

Figure 5.1 – Sausage Kolaches ready to bake.

Bake at 375° for about 18 minutes or until tops and bottoms are golden. Butter while still hot.

Cool on wire rack.

Delicious Authentic Czech Kolache Recipes

Chapter 6 - Left-Over Dough = Kačenky!

My mom would use leftover dough, tie it in a knot and bake it. She called these kačenky (KA-chen-kee) or "baby ducks" because that is what they looked like. She would sprinkle sugar on them or even ice them with a thin powdered-sugar icing and I loved them as a child.

1. Start with egg-sized pieces of dough.

2. Roll each piece of dough between your lightly floured hands until you have a strand of dough roughly 6 or 7 inches.

3. Tie a single knot in each strand of dough.

4. Place the knots on a buttered pan about 1 inch apart.

5. Butter the knots then set aside to allow to rise for about 30 minutes to 1 hour.

Delicious Authentic Czech Kolache Recipes

Figure 6.1 – Kačenky ready to bake

6. Bake at 375° about 18 minutes until tops are golden brown.

7. Butter the knots after removing from oven.

8. You can sprinkle them with sugar or a cinnamon-sugar mixture at this point.

9. Allow to cool on a wire rack.

Delicious Authentic Czech Kolache Recipes

Figure 6.2 – Baked Kačenky sprinkled with sugar

If you would like to watch me making Kačenky, you can see it on YouTube at…

http://youtu.be/aljVnqD1yuk

Delicious Authentic Czech Kolache Recipes

Chapter 7 – Videos

How to Make Kolache Dough
time = 10:37   http://youtu.be/K_gwIZkPACQ

How to Make Kolache Balls
time = 4:01   http://youtu.be/yVYcbhOP5Hs

How to Punch Down Kolache Balls
time = 2:07   http://youtu.be/G2M5vq0xq_0

Kolaches
time = 17:58   http://youtu.be/j9TgcHSC_hY

Sausage Kolaches
time = 9:05   http://youtu.be/TVBwWrW_5Gg

Filled Kolaches
time = 11:39   http://youtu.be/u3GK406AMGk

Kačenky
time = 6:10   http://youtu.be/aljVnqD1yuk

Dedication

Mary Sherek Tepera

4/30/1917 – 9/22/2011

I am happy to dedicate this book to my mom who taught me everything… not just how to bake kolaches.

Delicious Authentic Czech Kolache Recipes

My mom was born, the oldest surviving child, of Katherine and Frank Sherek near Jonah, TX. Czech families tended to settle near one another where they could continue their Czech customs and language.

Frank and Katherine moved to Schwertner, TX where they attended the Cornhill church and Mary went to the Cornhill School where she was taught English by nuns. Frank and Katherine had 9 more children.

Being the oldest of 10 children, Mom took over daily chores quickly and remembered standing on a chair in order to knead bread.

When mom became engaged to my dad, Louis Tepera, she found work chopping cotton so that she could pay for her wedding dress ($8).

Delicious Authentic Czech Kolache Recipes

Mom and Dad married and settled near Rogers, TX where they raised 7 children. Mom was determined that all of her children would graduate from high school and she worked long hours in the field next to my dad so that her children wouldn't miss school.

I guess Mom did what all Czech farm wives did back then... they all raised and grew their own food, sewed their own clothes, raised healthy children, and made their own kolaches, bread, and strudel!

It may seem like a lot of work to us but it was a work of love and joy to her. She said, looking back, they were poor but they didn't know it because everyone was poor back then.

Delicious Authentic Czech Kolache Recipes

She passed on to us a love of our Czech heritage and a love of life. She instilled in us honesty and faithfulness. She was always our greatest supporter. She encouraged us to pursue our dreams, to grow, to reach our potential. For this I am eternally grateful.

Delicious Authentic Czech Kolache Recipes

About The Author

Dorothy Tepera Palmer is proud to be 100% Czech and a second-generation American. She was raised in the Texas "Czech-Belt" where she learned to polka and waltz and bake kolaches as did all the other Czech "farm girls".

She is an experienced, professional baker and a retired Research Scientist. She and her husband reside near Galveston, TX. This is her first cookbook.

You can contact her at DPalmer@AggieNetwork.com

Dobrou chuť!